CW00758684

GALL
CENGAGE Learning

# Novels for Students, Volume 43

Project Editor: Sara Constantakis Rights Acquisition and Management: Robyn Young Composition: Evi Abou-El-Seoud Manufacturing: Rhonda Dover

Imaging: John Watkins

Product Design: Pamela A. E. Galbreath, Jennifer Wahi Digital Content Production: Allie Semperger Product Manager: Meggin Condino © 2013 Gale, Cengage Learning

For product information and technology assistance, contact us at **Gale Customer Support, 1-800-877-4253.**

For permission to use material from this text or product, submit all requests online at **www.cengage.com/permissions**.

Further permissions questions can be e-mailed to **permissionrequest@cengage.com**
While every effort has been made to ensure the reliability of the information presented in this publication, Gale, a part of Cengage Learning, does not guarantee the accuracy of the data contained herein. Gale accepts no payment for listing; and inclusion in the publication of any organization, agency, institution, publication, service, or individual does not imply endorsement of the editors or publisher. Errors brought to the attention of the publisher and verified to the satisfaction of the publisher will be corrected in future editions.

*Gale*
27500 Drake Rd.
Farmington Hills, MI, 48331-3535

ISBN-13: 978-1-4144-9486-9
ISBN-10: 1-4144-9486-6
ISSN 1094-3552

This title is also available as an e-book.

ISBN-13: 978-1-4144-9272-8
ISBN-10: 1-4144-9272-3
Contact your Gale, a part of Cengage Learning sales
representative for ordering information.

Printed in Mexico
1 2 3 4 5 6 7 17 16 15 14 13

# *The Guernsey Literary and Potato Peel Society*

## Mary Ann Shaffer and Annie Barrows

## 2008

## Introduction

*The Guernsey Literary and Potato Peel Pie Society* is an epistolary novel that takes place on Guernsey, an island off the English coast in the English Channel, between England and France. The events in the novel occur during the first nine months of 1946, just after the end of World War II and after the German occupation of the Channel Islands ended. While the central protagonist lives in London, her correspondents live on Guernsey.

Mary Ann Shaffer and Annie Barrows's novel shows the courage and fortitude of the people who lived on Guernsey during the five long years of German occupation. The islanders' humanity is revealed through their bravery in protecting one another from the ever-present threat of arrest and deportation. There is also a gentle humor in *The Guernsey Literary and Potato Peel Pie Society* that is evident in the creative character studies of some of the islanders' more eccentric and quirky characters. The islanders bond over a mutual love of books that they did not even know existed before the creation of the Guernsey Literary Society. Through their reading, the islanders are transported to worlds they might never have visited, or ever experienced.

*The Guernsey Literary and Potato Peel Pie Society* is Shaffer's first novel. She became ill and was unable to finish the final edits and rewrites that the publisher required. Shaffer's niece Annie Barrows completed the novel, which was published in 2008, after Shaffer's death.

The writing of *The Guernsey Literary and Potato Peel Pie Society* was a joint effort. Shaffer was the principal author, but when she became ill during the final stage of writing the novel, she asked her niece Annie Barrows to complete the novel for her.

Shaffer, whose maiden name was Fiery, was born on December 13, 1934, in Martinsburg, West Virginia. She graduated from Martinsburg High School in 1952 and attended Miami University of Ohio for two years but left without completing a degree. She married Dick Shaffer in 1958, and in 1962 the couple moved to Greenbrae, California. The couple had two daughters. Shaffer worked as an editor and in libraries and in bookstores for many years, but she always dreamed of writing a novel. Several times during her adult life, Shaffer would begin writing a mystery novel but never finished any of them. She loved telling stories but found it difficult to make the transition from telling a story to writing a story. She began writing *The Guernsey Literary and Potato Peel Pie Society* only after members of her writing group pushed her to start writing as a serious endeavor.

The genesis for *The Guernsey Literary and Potato Peel Pie Society* was a 1980 visit to England, when Shaffer decided to fly to Guernsey. Fog kept Shaffer stranded in the airport on Guernsey for seventy-two hours. She spent her time reading books from the airport gift shop, where almost all of the books told the story of the German occupation of Guernsey during World War II. Shaffer found the occupation of the Channel Islands fascinating history and bought nearly every book she could find.

Although she found the history of Guernsey compelling, it still took Shaffer more than twenty years to begin writing her novel and then only after encouragement from friends. Shaffer began writing the novel in 2003 and chose the epistolary format because it was one she enjoyed reading and that she thought would be easy to duplicate. By the time *The Guernsey Literary and Potato Peel Pie Society* was accepted for publication, Shaffer was ill with cancer and could not complete the revisions and additional writing the publisher required. She asked Barrows to help finish the book. Shaffer died of cancer February 16, 2008, before the novel's publication.

Barrows, the daughter of Shaffer's sister, Cynthia Fiery Barrows, was born in San Diego in 1962. She was raised in Northern California and graduated from the University of California, Berkeley, with a bachelor's degree in medieval history. Barrows also earned a master of fine arts from Mills College. Barrows lives in California with her husband and two daughters. After working as a book editor for several years, Barrows began writing books. Her first books–nonfiction for adults–were published under the name Ann Fiery. Barrows' first nonfiction book was *The Book of*

*Divination* (1999). This first book was soon followed by two additional works of nonfiction: *The Completely and Totally True Book of Urban Legends* (2001) and *At the Opera: Tales of the Great Operas* (2003).

In 2006, Barrows published the first of the *Ivy and Bean* children's book series. Nine children's books in this series were published between 2006 and 2012. The *Ivy and Bean* books have received numerous accolades, including being named one of the New York Public Library's 100 Titles for Reading and Sharing (2006), *Book Links* Best New Books for the Classroom (2006), *Kirkus Reviews* Best Children's Book (2006), *Booklist's* Best Books of 2007, and ALA Notable Children's Book (2007). The books were also nominated for the Kentucky Bluegrass Award (2008), North Dakota Flicker Tale Children's Book Award (2010–2011), and the Bluestem Award (2011). The *Ivy and Bean* books were not individually selected for these awards; instead, the series has been celebrated for excellence as a whole. In 2008, Barrows published a children's chapter book, *The Magic Half*, which was also nominated for several awards, including the Kentucky Bluegrass Award, the Mark Twain Award, the Virginia Readers' Choice, the Massachusetts Children's Book Award, the Maud Hart Lovelace Award, and the Sunshine State Young Readers' Award, all in 2011.

In 2007, Shaffer asked Barrows to help complete the required editing and rewrites for *The Guernsey Literary and Potato Peel Pie Society.*

Barrows, who had grown up listening to her aunt's stories and knew her storytelling style well, began working to finish the novel, which was published in the summer of 2008, after Shaffer had died. The Guernsey Literary and Potato Peel Pie Society is Barrows's first adult fiction book.

# Plot Summary

## *Part One*

### *JANUARY 1946*

The first few letters that open *The Guernsey Literary and Potato Peel Pie* Society are an exchange between Juliet Ashton and her publisher and friend, Sidney Stark. They are largely filled with idle chitchat about how dissatisfied Juliet is with her current activity, which consists of a book tour to promote and sell *Izzy Bickerstaff Goes to War*, a collection of the columns that Juliet wrote during the war. In response, Sidney offers vague encouragement about writing another book. Juliet also writes to her childhood friend Sophie Strachan about the destruction that Juliet sees during her book tour of postwar England.

# Media Adaptations

- An audiobook of *The Guernsey Literary and Potato Peel Pie Society*, with multiple unnamed readers, was released by Random House Audio in 2008.

- As of 2012, a film of *The Guernsey Literary and Potato Peel Pie Society* is under way, to be directed by Kenneth Branagh. The book is adapted by Don Roos, and filming is to begin in 2013 and will star Kate Winslet as Juliet Ashton.

---

While on the book tour, Juliet is accosted by a reporter, who badgers her about a broken engagement that occurred four years earlier. The near groom was killed in action only three months later, and obviously Juliet is sensitive about these events, since she throws a teapot at the offending journalist. The reason for the broken engagement is soon revealed. The day before the wedding, Juliet's fiancé packed up all her books and was in the midst of storing them in the basement, when she arrived home to find all her bookshelves filled with his athletic trophies. After a huge fight over the displacement of her books and about how little the couple actually had in common, Juliet and her fiancé broke off their engagement. The irony is that when her London home was later bombed, her books might have been safe in the basement, had she left them there.

During her book tour, Juliet also receives many bouquets of flowers from Mark Reynolds, a wealthy American publisher who seems to be courting Juliet. His purpose is not clear, but readers learn that he is very handsome and that many ladies find him difficult to resist. Since Juliet has never met Mark, his pursuit of her is both intriguing and romantic to Juliet, who is bored and without any real direction in her life.

Juliet receives her first two letters from Guernsey, from Dawsey Adams, who has found Juliet's name and address inside a used book and who, in his first letter, asks that Juliet help him find copies of Charles Lamb's writings. Juliet does find the requested Lamb books and makes sure that Dawsey receives them. In their correspondence, Juliet reveals that her home was bombed during the war and that she has now rented a less attractive apartment in London. Both Juliet and Dawsey are great lovers of books and reading.

In his second letter, Dawsey tells Juliet the story of the founding of the Guernsey Literary and Potato Peel Pie Society, which was organized on the spur of the moment after several of the Guernsey residents were stopped by German soldiers and had to explain why they were out after curfew. Dawsey's letter relates details about the shortage of food during the German occupation of Guernsey and the lack of war news as well. The Germans did not allow any letters, newspapers, magazines, or other written items to be imported during the war years.

## FEBRUARY 1946

The correspondence between Juliet and Dawsey continues with letters that reveal quite a lot about their respective lives. Juliet says that she was a writer during the war and that she wrote the Izzy Bickerstaff columns but that she is now going to write under her own name. Juliet also tells Dawsey that she has been asked to write a feature story for the *London Times* about the philosophical benefits of reading. Juliet asks Dawsey for help from him and the Guernsey Literary and Potato Peel Pie Society. In response, Amelia Maugery writes to Juliet to ask for references before she begins to write anything about the society. Amelia is concerned that the islanders not become objects of derision in any article that Juliet writes.

The two letters of reference that Amelia receives focus on Juliet's honesty and her love of books, although the letters also make clear that she can be reckless at times. Readers also learn that Juliet was orphaned and sent to live with an elderly uncle, who in turn sent her to a boarding school. After she receives the letters of reference, Amelia writes to Juliet to tell her more about the founding of the Guernsey Literary Society, which had to be transformed from a fictional book club to a real book club. Amelia explains how she and Elizabeth McKenna bought every book they could find and began lending them out to their neighbors. The plan was to make the Guernsey Literary Society an actual book club, just in case the German forces decided to check on the members' alibi for breaking curfew. Isola Pribby writes and tells Juliet about her passion for the Brontë sisters and how she came to love their books. Isola also explains that Elizabeth was arrested and deported after she was caught hiding a Polish slave worker.

Eben Ramsey then writes to Juliet and tells her about the day the Germans invaded the island and the more than thirty men, women, and children they killed. Eben also tells Juliet about the deprivation and hunger that everyone suffered during the years that the Germans occupied the island. At first, the islanders' diets consisted of just potatoes and turnips, but eventually there were no more potatoes to eat. They also had no fuel for heating their homes or candles for light. Eben's seven-year-old grandson, Eli, was sent to England to safety and only returned five years later, after the Germans left.

Juliet finally meets Mark Reynolds and discovers that he is quite handsome and polished, is accustomed to ordering people around, and is used to having his own way. He has read Juliet's book and has set out to impress her. She goes out with Mark several times and describes evenings spent at the cinema and at dinner parties and nights out dancing. She also mentions that he is an American and seems to have put the war behind him, as the British have not yet done.

# MARCH 1946

Juliet receives a letter from Adelaide Addison, who sits in judgment over her neighbors and considers most of them to be ill-bred, unintelligent, and scarcely capable of reading, much less actually belonging to, a true literary society. A letter from Clovis Fossey also arrives, in which he details how the Guernsey Literary and Potato Peel Pie Society and a book of poetry helped him win the love of a local widow.

Eben writes in a letter about the food rationing during the German occupation. He explains that the Germans kept track of every farm animal and every ounce of milk, all of the butter and eggs produced, and every fish caught. He tells Juliet that the island people learned tricks to fool the Germans, which is how they had a pig to eat the night they were almost caught and formed the Guernsey Literary and Potato Peel Pie Society.

Adelaide writes again and tells Juliet about Elizabeth's love for a German doctor and the child that she had after he left the island. Adelaide thinks Elizabeth's behavior was a disgrace. After Elizabeth was arrested and deported, the members of the Guernsey Literary Society decided to raise her baby, Kit, and everyone took turns caring for the child. Adelaide did not approve of any of these activities and pleads with Juliet not to use the people of Guernsey in the article she is writing.

John Booker also writes to Juliet and tells how he came to impersonate his employer, Lord Tobias, and how he chose to pretend to be a lord of the mansion. He had the help of Elizabeth and Amelia, who told him not to reveal his Jewish ancestry and to claim that he was a lord. Elizabeth and Amelia saved his life, as did reading the Roman philosopher Seneca, whose witty writings filled John's days.

In her last letter of March, Juliet writes to Sidney, who is in Australia visiting a friend and healing a broken leg. She tells him about the letters she has been exchanging with the people of Guernsey and that she wants to write a book about the people who spent the war years on the Channel Islands as prisoners of the Germans.

## APRIL 1946

Dawsey writes to Juliet and explains why some islanders were friendly to the Germans and how the food that they received in return helped feed their families. Dawsey also details how his friendship with Christian Hellman, the man whom Elizabeth loved, started. Dawsey writes about how the German doctor helped him carry saltwater for cooking to the older islanders, who could not fetch the water themselves. He tells Juliet how Christian drowned when his ship was bombed and sank in the Channel.

A letter from Amelia tells Juliet about how Adolf Hitler sent sixteen thousand Todt slave laborers to the Channel Islands to build fortifications and bunkers on the islands. Todt was the name of a German construction firm that depended on laborers captured in the countries that the Nazis invaded and conquered. Amelia asks Juliet to come to Guernsey and write a book about the war there.

A letter from Eben tells Juliet that the islanders never thought Germany would bother with the small Channel Islands, because their focus was on the larger prize of England. When the invasion seemed inevitable, people had to decide whether to send their children to England for safekeeping, but the decision was very difficult for parents, and not all children were sent.

Even as she receives more letters from the islanders, Juliet begins researching the history of Guernsey. In response to a request from Isola, Juliet describes her appearance, how she got her start writing, and many of the small details surrounding her life. Juliet tells Isola that she began writing professionally after she won an essay contest and her essay was published. The resulting fan letters led the *Daily Mirror* newspaper to offer her a job writing feature stories. This job eventually led the *Spectator* to offer her a regular position writing a humorous war column, which was the start of the Izzy Bickerstaff columns.

The final letters of April tell Juliet how Elizabeth slapped Adelaide across the face after she scared a group of children waiting to be evacuated. Juliet's suitor, Mark, continues his pursuit of her. His letters make clear that he cares little for her opinions or desires. He is accustomed to getting things done his way.

Juliet's first letter in May is to Mark, who is upset and jealous about the time she devotes to her friendship with Sidney and to the people of Guernsey. Mark has asked Juliet to marry him, and her reply that she needs time to think about it has angered him. Juliet writes to Sophie that when she did not immediately accept his proposal, Mark began shouting at her, reducing Juliet to tears. Juliet's letter to Sophie is a plea for advice concerning what to do about Mark. Should she drop her goals and marry Mark and be the ideal society wife he expects? Or should she stick to her career and not marry Mark? These are Juliet's questions as May begins. In her letter to Sidney, Juliet never mentions Mark but instead writes of how much she wants to go to Guernsey, meet the people who have been writing to her, and learn more about the German occupation.

The islanders are thrilled that Juliet plans to visit Guernsey and begin preparing for her visit. In their letters, they describe their efforts to find her housing and their plans for a welcome party. Even more people have been enticed to write to Juliet about their experiences during the occupation. An anonymous writer tells Juliet that the authorities in London ordered all feral dogs and cats, who had no owner, and all pets in excess of one per household to be destroyed. The reason for the order was that there was insufficient food on the island to feed so many dogs and cats. There was also insufficient food to feed either the islanders or the German soldiers. At one point near the end of the war, the German soldiers were so hungry they resorted to eating stray cats.

While the preparations for Juliet's arrival on Guernsey continue, Mark continues to implore her to forget her plans. His tone is increasingly condescending. Juliet is to stay in Elizabeth's cottage, which has been empty since she was arrested.

# Part Two

## MAY 1946

When Juliet arrives on Guernsey, she is greeted by many of the islander correspondents. She takes the time to describe each of them in a letter to Sidney. They are so warm and welcoming that Juliet's initial nervousness evaporates. The many letters that finish the month of May are written to Sidney and to his sister, Sophie. These letters are filled with Juliet's small observations of life on Guernsey and the lives of the people who live there. Juliet devotes her time to getting to know the island and the people, even as she continues to learn more about the German occupation of the Channel Islands. Juliet also bonds with four-year-old Kit, who spends much of her time with Juliet at Elizabeth's former cottage.

## JUNE 1946

The Guernsey Literary and Potato Peel Pie Society receives a letter from Remy Giraud, who was friends with Elizabeth while both were imprisoned at Ravensbrück concentration camp. Remy writes to tell Elizabeth's friends of her death at the camp. She describes the camp and the way the women lived and tells how Elizabeth was killed for defending another prisoner, who was being beaten. When Amelia and Dawsey learn of Elizabeth's death, they travel to Louviers, France, to convince Remy that she must journey to Guernsey, just as she and Elizabeth had planned before her death. After everyone learns of Elizabeth's death, Kit is told. Because Amelia was in France and then feels unwell upon her return, Kit stays with Juliet in Elizabeth's former cottage.

## *JULY 1946*

Sidney travels to Guernsey to meet all the people Juliet has been corresponding with and writing about for the previous six months. His observational skills are excellent, and it takes him no time at all to realize that Kit loves Juliet, that Juliet loves Kit, that Dawsey is very attracted to Juliet, and that Juliet is very attracted to Dawsey. When Isola wants to know whether Sidney and Juliet are in love and getting married, Sidney tells her that he is homosexual, which pleases Isola very much.

Sidney reads all of Juliet's interview notes and the letters she has received and tells her that Elizabeth needs to be at the center of her book about Guernsey. It is Elizabeth who was so instrumental in everyone's lives and is the focus of all the other islanders whose stories Juliet has been collecting.

Mark appears on the island at an inopportune moment, just as Juliet realizes that she wants Dawsey to kiss her and just as it appears he will. Mark is rude and condescending, and Juliet sends him packing back to London with a firm rejection of his marriage proposal. Unfortunately, Dawsey thinks Juliet is in love with Mark. Dawsey leaves for France without saying goodbye. His plan is to bring Remy to Guernsey to continue her recovery.

## *AUGUST 1946*

Remy has arrived, and everyone works hard to be cheerful and to help her convalesce. Life on the island continues, as do meetings of the Guernsey Literary Society, where people still read and discuss books. The ending of the war is no reason to abandon the literary society that has come to mean so much to everyone. Isola brings forth a collection of letters that her granny once received, and it is determined that they were written by Oscar Wilde, a fact that elicits a great deal of attention on and off the island. Dawsey continues to ignore Juliet, never speaking and barely looking at her. Juliet is blind to the fact that his new behavior toward her is tied to the appearance of Mark and to the notion that Juliet is in love with either Mark or Sidney. Meanwhile, Juliet is worried about Remy and a possible romance with Dawsey and wishes that Remy would return to France to recover.

## *SEPTEMBER 1946*

Juliet wants to adopt Kit and begins telling Amelia of her plans. Juliet knows that Kit loves and trusts her and also understands that both she and Kit need to remain on Guernsey. Juliet will not be returning to London when her book is completed.

Isola begins keeping a journal and writes that she is convinced that Dawsey loves Remy but is too shy to tell her. Remy is to leave for Paris, where she has plans to start her life over. Isola searches through Dawsey's home looking for evidence that he is in love with Remy so that he can declare himself before Remy leaves. All she finds is that he has been keeping photos and keepsakes that belong to Juliet. Isola still fails to understand, but when she tells Juliet what she found, Juliet does understand. She immediate goes to find Dawsey and asks him to marry her. He agrees. In her final letter, Juliet writes to Sidney to tell him that she is getting married right away and needs him to come to Guernsey on the following Saturday to give her away. Eben will be the best man, and Isola will be the maid of honor. Always one to take control, Juliet is marrying Dawsey immediately and is ready to start the next chapter of her life.

## Dawsey Adams

Dawsey is a pig farmer who lives on Guernsey. He is the first inhabitant of the island with whom Juliet corresponds. Dawsey facilitates the connections between Juliet and the other island inhabitants. He is a good man but socially inexperienced and shy. However, he is also very generous and willing to help others. His father died when he was eleven, and his mother had no time for him. Dawsey used to stutter and, as a result, is unsure of himself around other people. He has been alone and lonely most of his life. Because of the Guernsey Literary and Potato Peel Pie Society, Dawsey makes friends for the first time and learns to communicate with people. He is attracted to Juliet when he finally meets her but is too shy to declare his feelings. The experiences that result from his membership in the Guernsey Literary Society and his friendships with the group members help Dawsey assume a new strength that had been hidden previously. He is stronger and braver and more willing to take chances. At the end of the novel, Dawsey finally realizes that Juliet loves him as much as he loves her.

## Adelaide Addison

Adelaide is the island grump and a notable

elitist who cares more about social conventions than about people. She finds fault with everyone, including Elizabeth. She is not a part of the Guernsey Literary and Potato Peel Pie Society and thinks it a waste of time. Her role is to reveal details about each person's life that she thinks casts aspersions on his or her character. In truth, her letters reveal the writer to be a petty and judgmental woman, filled with bitterness.

## *Juliet Ashton*

Juliet is the protagonist in this novel. She is a writer and journalist, and, during World War II, she wrote a column for the *Spectator* using the pseudonym Izzy Bickerstaff. The column that she wrote was light and humorous, designed to take people's minds off the war. When the war ended, Juliet wanted to write something more serious. She is thirty-two when the novel begins, and in her first letters, she is quickly defined by her sense of humor and her unhappiness at being only a columnist. She yearns to be taken seriously as a writer. Through the letters that she writes, readers learn about Juliet's values and her efforts to create a life after her parents died in an automobile crash.

Juliet was orphaned at age twelve and attended boarding schools. She easily makes friends and is very loyal to them. She is used to being independent, which is why she is still unmarried when *The Guernsey Literary and Potato Peel Pie Society* begins. Juliet has a great deal of strength and resiliency and is capable of being good and loyal when called upon.

Juliet loves books, and thus her initial connection to Guernsey is established through a mutual love of books. The members of the Guernsey Literary and Potato Peel Pie Society are also great book lovers, and the initial exchange of letters focuses on the favorite books of each member. Juliet is determined to tell the story of the wonderful people of Guernsey and especially that of Elizabeth, whose love for her friends and neighbors and whose kindness toward everyone made her a focus for the islanders.

Throughout the novel, Juliet grows and changes, but her inner strength and compassion are always at the center of her humanity. She falls in love with the orphaned Kit and wants to adopt her. It takes Juliet a long time to become aware that she loves Dawsey, but once she understands that he loves her, she is willing to take control. She tells him that she loves him and asks him to marry her. Her independence is a big part of her strength.

## *Billee Bee*

Billee is Sidney's secretary, who, unbeknownst to Sidney, conspires with a disgraced journalist to steal the Oscar Wilde letters that Isola inherited from her granny. Billee completely underestimates the intelligence of the islanders and is caught with the stolen letters before she can escape from the island.

## John Booker

John is a former valet who assumed the identity of his employer, Lord Tobias, during the German occupation. When his wealthy employer left Guernsey just before the Germans invaded the island, John took over his employer's estate and pretended to be a man of wealth. He did so because his mother was Jewish. If he pretended to be a wealthy member of the British aristocracy, he could bluff his way out of revealing any kind of documentation that might require him to register as a Jew. Eventually, another islander turned him in, and John was shipped to a series of concentration camps, including Bergen-Belsen, in Germany. At the end of the war, John returned to Guernsey as soon as he was liberated from the concentration camp where he was imprisoned.

## Clovis Fossey

Clovis is a local farmer, who has never been one to read books. When he learns that women like poetry, he gets his first book of poetry, discovers that he loves it and William Wordsworth, and then wins the hand of the widow he has been courting.

## Remy Giraud

Remy was Elizabeth's friend at Ravensbrück concentration camp. Remy writes to the members of the Guernsey Literary and Potato Peel Pie Society after the war ends and tells Elizabeth's friends how she died. Once she is well enough, Remy visits Guernsey to recover. At the end of the novel, she leaves to return to Paris and continue her recovery.

## Christian Hellman

Christian was the German doctor with whom Elizabeth fell in love. He has been dead several years before Juliet receives her first letter from Guernsey. He is Kit's father. Unlike many of the other German occupiers, Christian was kind to the people on Guernsey and tried to make their lives easier during the wartime occupation. He was also a friend to Dawsey and to several of the islanders. He genuinely loved Elizabeth and wanted to marry her and return to Guernsey after the war but was killed when his transport ship was sunk in the Channel.

## Amelia Maugery

Amelia is everyone's mother figure on Guernsey; she is also sophisticated and wise. She is the first host of the Guernsey Literary and Potato Peel Pie Society and is highly regarded by her neighbors for her wise counsel. She befriends Juliet and is a sort of grandmother figure to Kit.

## Elizabeth McKenna

Elizabeth is not one of Juliet's correspondents. Her story is told by the other inhabitants of the island. Elizabeth was deported to a concentration camp and, when the novel begins, has been missing for several years. She was arrested after the Germans caught her hiding and feeding a teenage Polish slave worker. Because Elizabeth was a good friend to many of the people who live on Guernsey, her absence is an important part of their correspondence with Juliet. Elizabeth was kind and caring toward others and was always willing to help people. When she fell in love with a German doctor, some of her neighbors disapproved of her choice, but they still liked her. It was Elizabeth who dreamed up the Guernsey Literary and Potato Peel Pie Society, and it is her memory, even after her deportation, that unites many of the islanders. The islanders learn that Elizabeth was killed at the Ravensbrück concentration camp. Elizabeth is at the center of all the stories that people tell about the German occupation, and it is Elizabeth's story that Juliet decides to tell in the book she plans to write about the German occupation of Guernsey.

## Kit McKenna

Kit is Elizabeth's four-year-old daughter. Like her mother, Kit is loving and good. After Juliet visits Guernsey, Kit bonds with Juliet and begins to see Juliet as a mother figure. At the end of the novel, Juliet prepares to adopt Kit.

## Isola Pribby

Isola is the village eccentric. Through her activities, she provides much of the humor in the book. She loves to read romances and is passionate about the novels of the Brontë sisters. She describes herself as unattractive, with a large nose that has been broken and with wild hair that cannot be controlled. She cooks up many strange potions, but when Sidney sends her a book on phrenology—the reading of bumps on people's heads—Isola begins to "read" people's heads. Her insights are remarkably accurate. Isola's description of her appearance initially suggests the image of a witch, but her personality is gentle and caring toward others.

## Eben Ramsey

Eben is also a member of the Guernsey Literary and Potato Peel Pie Society. He describes himself as an elderly gentleman who has discovered that he loves to read Shakespeare. Eben is very observant and quite smart; as a result, he became a repository for small details about life on Guernsey during the German occupation. Eben is also the guardian of his twelve-year-old grandson, Eli, who was sent to England for safety when the island was initially occupied by the Germans. Like so many others on the island, Eben is a good friend to his neighbors and to Juliet.

## Eli Ramsey

Eli is Eben's grandson. He was sent to England at age seven and did not return to Guernsey until he was twelve years old. Both of his parents died during the war. Eli's mother and her new baby died the day the Germans bombed Guernsey. His father died in 1942, while fighting in World War II. Eli's actual last name is uncertain. His mother, Jane, was Eben's daughter, but his father's name is never provided.

## Mark Reynolds

Mark is an American publisher who courts Juliet. He is wealthy and handsome and offers Juliet a life of glamour and wealth. He is not a man who accepts no for an answer, and he is not pleased when Juliet tells him she needs time to think about his marital proposal. Mark wants Juliet as a sort of English trophy wife and cares little for her happiness. He has no interest in her writing and does not wish her to write or work. His idea of a marriage partner is someone devoted to him and his interests. Mark comes to Guernsey intending to storm the island and sweep Juliet off her feet and back to London. When Juliet declines his proposal and sends him back to London, Mark is very angry.

## Susan Scott

Susan is a minor character who accompanies Juliet on the book tour that opens *The Guernsey Literary and Potato Peel Pie Society*. She represents the publisher of Juliet's book and is expected to keep an eye on her charge. She occasionally writes to Juliet when she is on Guernsey.

## Sidney Stark

Sidney Stark is Juliet's publisher. He is also a childhood friend, although Sidney is ten years older than Juliet. The correspondence between Juliet and Sidney is central to much of the novel. Sidney is the clear voice of reason and the one friend Juliet can count on to be honest with her. His advice to Juliet is always focused on her well-being, which makes him a true friend. Like his sister, Sophie, Sidney functions as a sounding board for Juliet. He is capable of seeing what she does not see, which makes his advice especially valuable. Sidney does not like Mark and quickly understands that he would be a very bad match for Juliet. Sidney is homosexual and is not a romantic interest for Juliet. The letters that Juliet writes to Sidney are a primary source for readers to learn everything that Juliet is learning about the people and the island of Guernsey.

## Sophie Strachan

Sophie is Juliet's childhood friend from boarding school and also Sidney's younger sister. Juliet writes letters to Sophie but does not receive replies. As a result, readers do not really get to know Sophie's voice. Sophie functions as a sounding board for Juliet when she needs to work through something that is bothering her. The letters that Juliet writes to Sophie provide many of the details about Guernsey life, especially in the second half of the book, when Juliet is living on Guernsey.

## *Will Thisbee*

Will is one of the members of the Guernsey Literary and Potato Peel Pie Society. He wanted food at the meetings and was responsible for the inclusion of the potato peel pie in the title. He is a terrible cook but means well and often brings food to people's homes.

# Courage

In *The Guernsey Literary and Potato Peel Pie Society*, there are many examples of courage in how people dealt with the days before the German occupation, the actual occupation, and the year following the end of the war. Before the German invasion of Guernsey, parents had to decide whether to send their children to safety in England. It took enormous courage to send children to an unknown future, where they would be unable to contact their parents.

In creating the Guernsey Literary and Potato Peel Pie Society, Elizabeth was extraordinarily brave. She did not cower when confronted by German soldiers after being out after curfew. Although there were guns aimed at her head, she instinctively created a story that would save herself and her companions. When another islander found a young Polish slave laborer near death, he and Elizabeth made the decision to help the boy. Elizabeth had her own infant child, but she did not hesitate to step forward to help care for this teenage boy, who would die without her intervention. As a prisoner at Ravensbrück, Elizabeth chose to be a friend to another woman who desperately needed a friend in the camp. Remy's own experience and survival are tied to Elizabeth's friendship and support. Then when Elizabeth saw the beating of another woman, she stopped the guard from beating the woman and even seized the weapon and began to beat the guard. Elizabeth was executed for her bravery. Her choice to face her enemies and to act out of humanity and not cowardice was one of her most important characteristics. It is Elizabeth's courage that unites the islanders and infuses them with the courage to survive the occupation of the island during war.

Elizabeth is not the only example of a courageous person whose actions helped the islanders survive the German occupation of Guernsey. The people who attended the Guernsey Literary Society initially did so to protect Elizabeth's story and as a way to fight the effects of German intimidation. People hid food and devised ways to fake a pig's death as a means to provide extra food. Everything that the islanders did during the five years of German occupation reveals their bravery in the face of real and significant danger.

## *Humanity*

Although there is little doubt about the humanity of many of the islanders, which is aptly displayed by their loyalty to and care of one another in the face of danger, some of the German soldiers are revealed to possess humanity as well. Kit's father, Christian, helped Dawsey bring water to the islanders unable to carry their own cooking water. In addition, some of the German soldiers "accidentally" let potatoes and oranges fall from German transport trucks, so that the children chasing the trucks could gather up the extra food to eat. One German soldier delivered medicine to an islander whose child was sick. The examples of the German soldiers' humanity make clear that the enemy was not always a simple stereotype of evil. The more humane German soldiers are a reminder that even in war the enemy can have good and humane soldiers within their ranks.

## *Loyalty*

The islanders are very loyal to one another. When Juliet first begins to consider writing about the German occupation of Guernsey, the islanders decide that she must prove that her intentions are good. She must be a person of character, and she must be trustworthy, since the islanders do not wish to be a topic of derision. Both Elizabeth, who arrived as a child, and Juliet, who arrives to write a book, are strangers who are taken into the islanders' lives and who become part of the community. The islanders are protective of one another and loyal to their island family.

# Topics for Further Study

- Research the women's prison at Ravensbrück. Search for photos, illustrations, and video taken of the camp and prepare a multimedia presentation in which you carefully integrate photos, video, and quotations from survivors' memoirs. Explain to your classmates what the experience at Ravensbrück was like for the prisoners who were sent there.

- Based on your readings of *The Guernsey Literary and Potato Peel Pie Society*, write an imaginary obituary for either Juliet or Dawsey in which you relate his or her history, as you know it from reading the novel, and your prediction of how either of their futures plays out over the fifty years following their marriage. Post the obituary on a blog and allow classmates to comment.

- Research the Channel Islands (primarily Jersey, Guernsey, Alderney, and Sark), which have a rich lifestyle based on both their British and French heritages. Prepare an oral presentation in which you discuss the French aspects and the British aspects of life on the islands and how the islanders have adapted to and incorporated two such distinct cultures into their lives.

- Research the German occupation of the Channel Islands during World War II and then pretend that you lived there as a teenager. Write your own short story about what the experience would have been like. Write your story as a series of eight to ten letters to a friend who lives elsewhere. Describe the island, the people you know, and the events that are happening around you. Your story has to be long enough to incorporate events and your personal history, including that of your family.

- *Island at War* is a British miniseries

that aired in England in 2004 and was then shown on PBS's Masterpiece in 2005. This miniseries focuses on the German occupation of the Channel Islands. Watch the first episode, "Eve of the War," and write an essay in which you compare the information included in the episode with information from *The Guernsey Literary and Potato Peel Pie Society*. Note both the factual consistencies and inconsistencies.

- The novel *Code Talker: A Novel about the Navajo Marines of World War Two* (2005), by Joseph Bruchac, focuses on two Navajo teenagers whose experiences in the Pacific in the war against Japan were very different from those of the people of the Channel Islands. Read this novel and write an essay in which you compare the roles of the islanders on Guernsey with the activities of the Navajo code talkers. Each group was active in resisting the enemy and aiding the war effort. In your essay, consider which experiences are similar and which experiences are different.

- Potato peel pie, as it might have been cooked during World War II, contains potatoes, beets, and milk.

Preheat an oven to 375 degrees. Wash and dry two or three potatoes. Peel the potatoes and line a nine-inch pie plate with the peelings. Peel and trim one beet. Boil the potatoes and the beet for about fifteen minutes (until they can be pierced with a fork); then drain and mash, adding two tablespoons of milk. Fill the pie pan with the mashed potato and beet mixture. Bake at 375 degrees for fifteen minutes or until browned (being careful not to waste your fuel ration). Report to your classmates how the pie tastes.

---

Elizabeth was especially loyal to the people of Guernsey. She created the Guernsey Literary and Potato Peel Pie Society to save her friends' lives, but she also made it a reality. She helped find the books for the literary society, made sure that all her friends chose one, and then organized the twice-a-month meetings. When Elizabeth was arrested, her friends stepped forward to care for and raise her daughter, Kit. They cared and continue to care for this child as if she were their own. Because Elizabeth formed the Guernsey Literary Society to protect her friends, Kit has a family to raise her in her mother's absence. It is Elizabeth who painted a portrait of John as Lord Tobias and who fabricated the story of John as the disguised lord to save his life, because John's mother was Jewish and John would himself have had to register as a Jew. While at Ravensbrück, Elizabeth accepted the punishment for a stolen potato, even though she did not steal the potato. Her loyalty was to her fellow prisoners.

Juliet has her own loyal friends, who constitute her family. Although Juliet's parents were killed when she was twelve years old, Sophie and Sidney took her into their lives and became family for her. Readers never see the letters from Sophie, but Juliet's letters to her friend make the closeness of their relationship obvious. When Juliet is unsure about the choices she is making and the nature of her feelings, she writes to Sophie for advice. The same is true of Juliet's relationship with Sidney. He offers her advice and guides her career. When she is going to be married, it is Sidney who will fly to Guernsey to give away the bride.

# Style

## *Epistolary Novel*

The epistolary novel is one written entirely in letter form. The narrative of the novel is advanced through a series of letters written by one or more characters. The advantage of an epistolary novel is that the author is able to provide several points of view. The narration is not limited to one voice but can instead provide multiple voices and stories. In *The Guernsey Literary and Potato Peel Pie Society*, the reader learns the story of the German occupation of Guernsey during World War II. The story is told from many different perspectives, which also helps the reader grasp the complexity of the five-year occupation. For example, Juliet receives several letters describing the creation of the Guernsey Literary and Potato Peel Pie Society. Each letter adds slightly more information about the event, with each writer including a description as he or she remembers it.

## *Historical Fiction*

Historical fiction tells a story that is set in a historical period different from the one in which the author lives. In historical fiction, the setting can be one of the most important elements in the story. The events and the characters' responses depend on the location and time in which the novel is set. In *The*

*Guernsey Literary and Potato Peel Pie Society*, the time covers the years of World War II and the year immediately after the war ended. The events that occurred on the Channel Islands during the German occupation are the focus of the novel. The historical novel reconstructs a period in time so that readers are able understand the events. The persons depicted might be fictional, but the setting and events are basically accurate to the place and time. *The Guernsey Literary and Potato Peel Pie Society* reconstructs the invasion of Guernsey by the Germans and their occupation of the island. Although the actual islanders in the novel are fictional, the characters reveal the basic events surrounding the takeover, which are true.

## *The Channel Islands*

The Channel Islands are located off the coast of Normandy, closer to France than to England. Still, the islanders have always considered themselves to be English, rather than French. Originally the Channel Islands were part of Normandy, when William of Normandy conquered England in 1066 and became the English King William I. When William's son, Henry I, seized the Duchy of Normandy in 1106, the Channel Islands became part of England. Although the Duchy of Normandy was subsequently lost from English possession in 1204, the Channel Islands have continued to be a part of England, as self-governing possessions. Eight inhabited islands belonging to the Channel Islands; according to size from largest to smallest, the five main islands are Jersey, Guernsey, Alderney, Herm, and Sark.

The Channel Islands are considered to be dependent territories of the Crown. The islands are self-governed, under the authority of two bailiwicks, one each for Guernsey and Jersey. All the main islands except Jersey are in the Bailiwick of Guernsey. The islands have their own legal, fiscal, and administrative systems. Although the islands are essentially self-governing, primary legislation is approved by the queen's privy council.

Great Britain is responsible for defense and international relations. While the Channel Islands have adopted British laws and the residents consider themselves British subjects, their cuisine has traditionally been French, notwithstanding the potato peel pie described in *The Guernsey Literary and Potato Peel Pie Society*.

# Compare & Contrast

- **1940s:** In 1939, as war seems increasingly certain, the British government evacuates 1.5 million children from London. There will be two more evacuations of children during the course of the war.
  **Today:** Children are no longer singled out for evacuations in Britain; instead, efforts are made to evacuate entire families, as in the case of flooding in Wales in 2012. Fears of terrorism can lead to mass evacuations, as was the case in July 2005, when twenty thousand people were evacuated from Birmingham, owing to a bomb scare.

- **1940s:** Food rationing begins in Britain. Meat, butter, bacon, cheese, milk, eggs, sugar, and several other foods are all rationed. People are urged to eat potatoes and carrots. Everyone is provided with ration books. Because every person suffers equally, there is little complaining about the rationing of food.

**Today:** Food insecurity is a huge issue in many countries, where food shortages are a result of war and drought. Even today, food insecurity is not unheard of in Great Britain. In 2012, the price of food increased nearly 5 percent over the previous year. While this increase may not seem onerous, inflation coupled with the economic recession has made hunger a reality for many British citizens.

- **1940s:** In December 1941, British women are drafted into the armed forces. Unmarried women in their twenties serve in the military, police, and fire services throughout the war. Older women are drafted to work in factories.

  **Today:** Although many women have died and continue to die as a result of combat in the war in Afghanistan, official British policy is that women are not combat troops. The Ministry of Defense argued in 2010 that allowing women to be combat troops would be distracting to male combat troops.

Many notable writers have visited the islands, including Sir Walter Raleigh, Anthony Trollope, and George Eliot. Victor Hugo spent sixteen years living in exile on Jersey and then on Guernsey, where he finished writing *Les Misérables*. Juliet's decision to write a book about Guernsey is in keeping with the Channel Islands' literary past.

## *German Occupation of the Channel Islands*

On June 15, 1940, officials in London decided that the Channel Islands had no strategic importance and that Great Britain would not defend the islands from a German invasion. Four days later, on June 19, parents were advised to send their children to Great Britain for safety. People were given only a few hours to decide whether they wanted to evacuate their children or keep them at home on the islands. Children, mothers of small children, and schoolteachers were the first to be evacuated. The first boat left Guernsey on June 20, 1940. On June 28, German forces began bombing Guernsey. During the bombing, thirty-four islanders were killed and another sixty-seven were injured. The first German troops landed on Guernsey on June 30, 1940. Nine people were killed on the island of Jersey, which was also bombed. The neighboring island of Alderney had already been almost entirely evacuated. By the time that German troops arrived ashore only twelve civilians remained there. Germans took advantage of the abandonment of

Alderney and established four concentration camps on the island. The small island of Sark was similarly invaded, with a German contingent of only ten soldiers. Herm, the smallest of the main Channel Islands, received a German visit, but no soldiers were stationed there.

As was common in other occupied territories, the German command established a civilian governing council designed to maintain order. There were not many Jewish citizens remaining on the islands. Many had already evacuated, but twelve Jews on Jersey and four on Guernsey registered with the Nazi commander. By 1941, persecution of Jewish residents was under way, and the first Jewish citizens were deported to concentration camps in April 1942. Initially food and other supplies were delivered from France. In the first few years, food shortages were not especially severe. Adolf Hitler was convinced that the British would try to retake the Channel Islands and ordered that impregnable barriers be built. Todt slave laborers were imported to built the barricades, and it is estimated that four of every ten died. The occupation ended May 9, 1945, with the surrender of the German commandant to British forces. Liberation Day is still celebrated every May 9 on Guernsey.

# Critical Overview

*The Guernsey Literary and Potato Peel Pie Society* has received a great deal of attention from critics. Among the many critics who reviewed the book is Craig Wilson, who writes in USA Today that Shaffer has "produced ... a charming book" of letters. Wilson notes that booksellers like the book and that the historical setting is interesting, as are the eccentric characters who populate the novel. Wendy Smith writes in the *Washington Post that The Guernsey Literary and Potato Peel Pie Society* is not quite perfect. There are a few improbabilities, such as a book club where all the members actually read good literature and not "trashy thrillers." Still, Smith points out that these minor problems can be ignored as readers relish a novel that "is a sweet, sentimental paean to books and those who love them."

Although the review in *People* magazine was brief, the critics responsible for reviewing books did choose *The Guernsey Literary and Potato Peel Pie Society* as a People Pick in August 2008. These three critics—Moira Bailey, Clarissa Cruz, and Oliver Jones—call *The Guernsey Literary and Potato Peel Pie Society* "a jewel." Later in the same review, they write that "the book combines quirky and delightful characters with fascinating history, bringing alive the five-year occupation of Guernsey." In the final sentence, the three critics call *The Guernsey Literary and Potato Peel Pie*

*Society* a "poignant and keenly observed" novel with romance and love that is rich in "the immeasurable sustenance to be found in good books and good friends." Equally enthusiastic is Yvonne Zipp, critic for the *Christian Science Monitor*. After first writing that people who love books really love books about books, Zipp compliments the "enchanting" discussions about "authors from Catullus to Shakespeare." Zipp labels *The Guernsey Literary and Potato Peel Pie Society* a "labor of love" that "shows on almost every page."

As might be expected for a novel set in wartime Britain, the London newspapers were especially enthusiastic. In a notice printed in the *Guardian*, reviewer Stevie Davies focuses on the characters who populate this novel. Davies writes that the inhabitants of Guernsey are commemorated as "beautiful spirits who pass through our midst and hunker undercover through brutal times." According to Davies, these characters emerge from history as eccentric and kind and are "a comic version of the state of grace." Although the people of Guernsey suffer during the German occupation of their island, the evil of their German oppressors never overpowers the innate decency of the islanders. As for Shaffer's writing, Davies calls it "delicately offbeat, self deprecating," and "exquisitely turned." Shaffer's recreation of history is, Davies writes, especially effective at recreating the period of the London Blitz.

Laura Thompson's review of *The Guernsey Literary and Potato Peel Pie Society* for the London newspaper *Telegraph* initially focuses on the novel's protagonist, calling Juliet's voice "original and delightful." Like Smith in her *Washington Post* review, Thompson does not think the book perfect. This reviewer suggests that the plotting in the second half of the book is not as strong as in the first half and that the epistolary format is less effective after Juliet arrives on Guernsey; however, these weaknesses are not sufficient to distract from the book's many other strengths. According to Thompson, *The Guernsey Literary and Potato Peel Pie Society* has "substance beneath the delicious froth." This novel, writes Thompson, "is funny" and "moving." Thompson joins many other reviewers who continue to find much to enjoy in Shaffer and Barrow's novel.

# What Do I Read Next?

- Annie Barrows's children's novel *The Magic Half* (2009) is a story about a non-twin in a family of twins who discovers that she really does have a twin who lived in 1935.

- *Jersey under the Jack-Boot* (1992), by R.C.G. Maugham, is a nonfiction, first-person account of life on one of the Channel Islands after the German invasion of 1940.

- *Life in Occupied Guernsey: The Dairies of Ruth Ozanne 1940–1945* (2012), edited by William Parker, provides an eyewitness account of the German occupation of Guernsey. These diaries capture both the happy times for islanders and the deprivation of wartime shortages of food and fuel.

- *84 Charing Cross Road* (1970) is a story told through a collection of letters exchanged between Helene Hanff, who lived in New York, and a London bookseller whose establishment was located at 84 Charing Cross Road. The correspondence covers twenty years, beginning in 1949. Filled with a love for books, the letters end in 1969, when the London correspondent, Frank Doel, dies. Unlike an epistolary novel, these letters are not fictional. *84 Charing Cross Road* is a wonderful complimentary pairing to *The Guernsey Literary and Potato Peel Pie Society*, with their joint focus on a love of books.

- Peter Lihou's novel *Rachel's Shoe* (2010) is a young-adult novel set on one of the Channel Islands during World War II. This novel traces the lives of two teenagers into the 1970s to solve a mystery that began during the German occupation of the island.

- Arnold Griese's novel *The Wind Is Not a River* (1997) is written for middle-school students. The book focuses on the lives of two Native American children hiding from the Japanese army, which has captured and occupied their Attu village on the largest of the Alaskan Aleutian Islands, then a US territory.

- *Shattered: Stories of Children and War* (2003), by Jennifer Armstrong, is a collection of twelve short stories about children trying to survive war. The stories cover a vast period of time and distance, beginning during the American Civil War and continuing up to the war in Afghanistan.

- Alice Walker's novel *The Color Purple* (1982) is another modern example of epistolary fiction. This book tells the story of a young black woman, Celie, who finds that her inner strength is what she needs to survive racism and physical abuse in the American South during the first forty years of the twentieth century.

# Sources

Amos, Deborah, "Tales of a Nazi-occupied British Isle in 'Guernsey,'" Interview with Annie Barrows, National Public Radio website, July 29, 2008, http://www.npr.org/templates/transcript/transcript.ph storyId=93018411 (accessed July 16, 2012).

Bailey, Moira, Clarissa Cruz, and Oliver Jones, "Picks and Pans Review: Letters from a Troubled Isle," in *People*, Vol. 70, No. 6, August 11, 2008, http://www.people.com/people/archive/article/0,,202 (accessed July 16, 2012).

"British Police Order Evac of Central Birmingham District," in *USA Today*, July 9, 2005, http://usatoday30.usatoday.com/news/world/2005-07-09-birmingham-evac_x.htm (accessed September 30, 2012).

"The Channel Islands," *Island at War*, PBS website, http://www.pbs.org/wgbh/masterpiece/islandatwar/is (accessed July 20, 2012).

Cohen, Frederick E., "The Jews in the Islands of Jersey, Guernsey and Sark during the German Occupation 1940–1945," in *Journal of Holocaust Education*, Vol. 6, No. 1, 1997, pp. 27–81.

Courtenay-Thompson, Fiona, and Kate Phelps, eds., *The 20th Century Year by Year*, Barnes & Noble, 1998, pp. 142, 147, 149, 151.

Cummings, Angela, "Martinsburg Native Authors Heralded Book," in *Martinsburg Journal*, August

17, 2008, http://www.journal-news.net/page/content.detail/id/509545/Martinsburg-native-authors-heralded-book.html (accessed July 16, 2012).

Davies, Stevie, Review of *The Guernsey Literary and Potato Peel Pie Society*, in *Guardian*, August 8, 2008, http://www.guardian.co.uk/books/2008/aug/09/fictio (accessed July 12, 2012).

"Genocides, Politicides, and Other Mass Murder Since 1945, with Stages in 2008," Genocide Watch website, www.genocidewatch.org/images/GenocidesandPolit (accessed July 20, 2012).

"German Occupation of the Channel Islands," BBC History website, http://www.bbc.co.uk/history/topics/occupation_cha (accessed July 20, 2012).

Glennon, Lorraine, ed., *The 20th Century*, JG Press, 1999, pp. 298–301.

Grant, George, "Why Food Security Is Not Just a Problem for the Third World," in *Telegraph*, April 24, 2012, http://www.telegraph.co.uk/news/uknews/9224240/\food-security-is-not-just-a-problem-for-the-Third-World.html (accessed September 30, 2012).

Grossman, Lev, "Temptation Island," in *Time*, July 24, 2008, http://www.time.com/time/magazine/article/0,9171,1826283,00.html (accessed July 16, 2012).

Harmon, William, and Hugh Holman, *A Handbook to Literature*, 11th ed., Prentice Hall, 2009, pp. 95–96, 205–206, 270, 420–22, 508.

"Interview with Annie Barrows," LitLovers Online website, http://www.litlovers.com/reading-guides/13-fiction/406-guernsey-literary-and-potato-interview (accessed July 16, 2012).

Jennings, Peter, and Todd Brewster, "Over the Edge," in *The Century*, Doubleday, 1998, pp. 215–30.

"Jews of the Channel Islands," Holocaust Research Project website, http://www.holocaustresearchproject.org/nazioccupa (accessed July 20, 2012).

McAuliff, Michael, "Women Allowed in Combat under Senate Defense Bill," in *Huffington Post*, May 24, 2012, http://www.huffingtonpost.com/2012/05/24/women-combat-senate-defense-bill_n_1543763.html (accessed July 20, 2012).

Norton-Taylor, Richard, "Women Still Banned from Combat Roles after Ministry of Defence Review," in *Guardian*, November 29, 2010, http://www.guardian.co.uk/uk/2010/nov/29/women-combat-ban-remains (accessed September 30, 2012).

"The Occupation of the Channel Islands 1940–45," Heritage Guernsey website, http://www.heritageguernsey.com/historical-guernsey/ (accessed July 20, 2012).

Shaffer, Mary Ann, and Annie Barrows, *The Guernsey Literary and Potato Peel Pie Society*, Dial Press, 2008.

Smith, Wendy, "The Resistance," in *Washington Post*, August 3, 2008, http://www.washingtonpost.com/wp-dyn/content/article/2008/07/31/AR2008073102685.h (accessed July 12, 2012).

Thompson, Laura, Review of *The Guernsey Literary and Potato Peel Pie Society*, in *Telegraph*, August 30, 2008, http://www.telegraph.co.uk/culture/books/fictionrevi The-Guernsey-Literary-and-Potato-Peel-Pie-Society-by-Mary-Ann-Shaffer.html (accessed July 12, 2012).

Todorov, Tzvetan, "What Is Literature For?," in *New Literary History*, Vol. 38, No. 1, Winter 2007, pp. 13–32.

Wilson, Craig, "'Potato Peel Pie' Has Ingredients for Success," in *USA Today*, July 31, 2008, http://www.usatoday.com/life/books/news/2008-07-29-potato_N.htm (accessed July 16, 2012).

Zipp, Yvonne, Review of *The Guernsey Literary and Potato Peel Pie Society*, in Christian Science Monitor, July 28, 2008, http://www.csmonitor.com/Books/Book-Reviews/2008/0728/the-guernsey-literary-and-potato-peel-society (accessed July 12, 2012).

# Further Reading

Baer, Elizabeth R., and Myrna Goldenberg, eds., *Experience and Expression: Women, the Nazis, and the Holocaust*, Wayne State University Press, 2003.

> This text contains a collection of essays that focus on the experiences of women during the Holocaust. Several of the essays examine the ways in which women nurtured one another and thus enabled one another to survive.

Baines, Valerie, *Guernsey Sketchbook*, Book Guild, 2001.

> This book is a collection of sketches and watercolor prints that cover the author's forty years of visits to Guernsey.

Batiste, Rob, *Guernsey's Coast*, Guernsey Books, 2010.

> This book is a collection of essays, with many accompanying photographs, that explore the coastline of Guernsey.

Bunting, Madeleine, *The Model Occupation: The Channel Islands under German Rule* 1940–1945, Random House, 2004.

> Bunting's book is a sociological

study of how people react when living in an occupied territory. Bunting's portrait of the islanders is not always flattering. The focus on islanders as Nazi collaborators is not a popular view for the people of the Channel Islands.

De Gaulle Anthonioz, Geniviev, *The Dawn of Hope: A Memoir of Ravensbrück and Beyond*, Arcade, 1999.

This memoir by a member of the French resistance recounts her life as a political prisoner at Ravensbrück, the women's concentration camp in Germany.

Dwork, Deborah, ed., *Voices and Views: A History of the Holocaust*, Jewish Foundation for the Righteous, 2002.

This text provides an unusual historical account because it is formatted as a collection of personal essays that explore both the events of the Holocaust and the impact and meaning of this period of history.

Lang, Suzanne, *Displaced Donkeys: A Guernsey Family's War*, Pinknote Press, 2009.

This memoir tells the story of one family's decision to send their children to England. Families were given just twenty-four hours to decide whether to send their children to safety and whether to send them alone or with their mothers; likewise they had to choose whether fathers should also evacuate to join the British armed forces to defend England against invasion.

Rittner, Carolm and John K. Roth, eds., *Different Voices: Women and the Holocaust*, Paragon House, 1993.

This book is an anthology divided into three separate sections. The first section contains memoirs written by Jewish women who experienced the Holocaust. The second section provides a collection of essays that interpret the events of the period, from racism to resistance to moral choice. The final section contains essays that reflect on the events of the Holocaust.

Turner, Barry, *Outpost of Occupation: The Nazi Occupation of the Channel Islands*, 1940–1945, Aurum Press, 2010.

This account of the German occupation of the Channel Islands is rich in first-person testimonies by the people who were present on the Channel Islands at the time. It is a serious but readable historical account of the German occupation of the Channel Islands during World War II.

# Suggested Search Terms

Mary Ann Shaffer AND The Guernsey Literary and Potato Peel Pie Society Annie Barrows AND The Guernsey Literary and Potato Peel Pie Society Mary Ann Shaffer AND Guernsey visit Shaffer and Barrows AND epistolary novels Channel Islands AND Jewish deportations Channel Islands AND World War II

Guernsey AND German Occupation

Channel Islands AND Todt prisoners

Lightning Source UK Ltd.
Milton Keynes UK
UKHW021147190123
415622UK00014B/949